21st Century Skills **INNOVATION LIBRARY**

MINECRAFT
Beginner's Guide

CHERRY LAKE PUBLISHING • ANN ARBOR, MICHIGAN

by James Zeiger

A Note to Adults: Please review the instructions for the activities in this book before allowing children to do them. Be sure to help them with any activities you do not think they can safely complete on their own.

A Note to Kids: Be sure to ask an adult for help with these activities when you need it. Always put your safety first!

Published in the United States of America by Cherry Lake Publishing
Ann Arbor, Michigan
www.cherrylakepublishing.com

Reading adviser: Marla Conn, Read With Me Now
Photo Credits: Page 5, © Bloomua/Shutterstock.com; page 6, © Press
Association via AP Images; page 13, © urbanbuzz/Shutterstock.com;
all others, James Zeiger.

Library of Congress Cataloging-in-Publication Data
Zeiger, James, author.
  Minecraft beginner's guide / by James Zeiger.
     pages cm. — (21st Century Skills Innovation Library) (Unofficial guides)
  Audience: Grades 4 to 6.
  Includes bibliographical references and index.
  ISBN 978-1-63470-520-2 (lib. bdg.) — ISBN 978-1-63470-640-7 (pbk.) —
ISBN 978-1-63470-580-6 (pdf) — ISBN 978-1-63470-700-8 (ebook)
1. Minecraft (Game)—Juvenile literature. 2. Computer games—Juvenile
literature. I. Title.
  GV1469.M55Z45 2016
  793.93'2—dc23   2015032305

Cherry Lake Publishing would like to acknowledge the work of The Partnership
for 21st Century Skills. Please visit www.p21.org for more information.

Printed in the United States of America
Corporate Graphics
January 2016

Contents

Chapter 1

What Is *Minecraft?*

magine a world where everything is made of blocks. There are block chickens, block cows, and block spiders. Even your body is made of blocky shapes. This world has huge mountains to climb and deserts to travel across. It also has vast oceans to swim in and dark caves to explore. You have the power to turn this land into anything you want. What should you do? You can build a mansion to live in or craft armor

If you want to live in a castle in *Minecraft*, all you have to do is build one!

Minecraft is one of the most popular video games ever created.

and weapons to defend against creatures of the night. You can stock up on supplies by mining **ore** or farming crops. Your adventure is up to you. It is limited only by your imagination.

This world is exactly what you'll find when you start up a new game of Minecraft. Created by Swedish game developer Markus Persson and his team at Mojang, Minecraft is one of the world's most popular video games. More than 70 million copies have been sold to date. Thousands of the game's biggest fans even gather each year at an event called MineCon.

Meet the Creator

Markus Persson, better known to his fans as "Notch," created the earliest version of *Minecraft* entirely by himself. He originally saw the game as a project to work on for fun. However, once he released a version online, it quickly gained popularity. Persson formed a company called Mojang and hired other people to help him improve the game. Over the years, *Minecraft* has become one of the most successful video games of all time.

Minecraft has two main modes to choose from. In Survival mode, you can challenge yourself by building your world from scratch, with only a map to guide you. You must gather all your own resources from the world. You must also survive the nights when enemies called creepers come around.

Or you can take off the restraints and play in Creative mode. This mode is the ultimate crafter's

Dangerous enemies roam the world of *Minecraft* at night.

playhouse. In Creative mode, everything in *Minecraft* is available to you at any time. There is no need to gather resources or fend off attacks. You can simply build whatever you want.

Which mode will you play? As with most things in *Minecraft*, the choice is yours!

7

Chapter 2

The Basics

Before we get started with the fun stuff, let's learn a few basic rules of *Minecraft*. Just as in real life, the *Minecraft* world has day and night cycles, different types of environments, and **precipitation**. Daytime in *Minecraft* lasts 10 real-life minutes. Sunrise and sunset each last one and a half minutes, and night lasts seven.

Load up *Minecraft* and start a new game. Once it's loaded, take a look at your heads-up display. This is the

You can explore deserts, forests, and much more in *Minecraft*.

Quick Tip: Stackable Items

There is a limit to the amount of tools and resources you can carry in the game. This is determined by your **inventory**. You can carry 27 different items in your backpack and nine more in your hands.

Many items, such as wood blocks or coal, are stackable up to 64 times for one slot. This means a whole group of the same item only takes up one space in your inventory. Once you have more than 64 items of the same type, they will simply stack in another slot. Tools, such as pickaxes or swords, are not stackable.

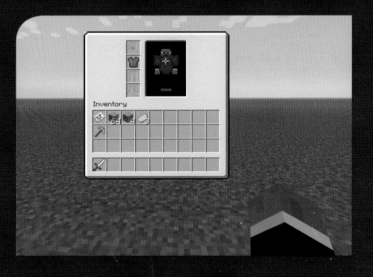

information that is displayed at the top of the screen, above the game world itself. The green number in the middle of your bars is your experience level. As you mine and craft items, you gain experience points. Once you gain enough points, your level will go up. The green bar underneath your experience level shows how close you are to the next level. Reaching higher levels will allow you to create stronger items later in the game.

To the right of your experience level is your food bar. If you are just starting, it should show 10 chicken legs. This is possibly the most important bar in the game. You need to pay close attention to it as you play. Certain actions will cause your food bar to deplete. These include sprinting, swimming, jumping, and breaking blocks. You can refill the bar by eating food. It is important to bring plenty of food along with you on your outings! When your food bar reaches three chicken legs or lower, you will no longer be able to sprint. This makes it a lot more difficult to get away from enemies.

Your health is indicated by the heart-shaped units to the left of your experience level. Taking damage

Quick Tip: How to Swim

You may encounter lakes and oceans during your *Minecraft* adventures. When in water, the Jump action will cause you to swim upward. Holding the Jump action will keep you on the surface. From there you can move in whichever direction you like.

Keep a close eye on your food and health as you play.

from enemies or fire will lower your health. So will falling from high places. Your health bar will **regenerate** slowly as long as your food bar is at eight units or higher. As a result, it is important to not let your food bar dip below eight units whenever possible. Eating food does not directly affect your health bar, but it will fill your food bar. This allows your health to regenerate naturally.

When your health points reach zero, your character dies. Upon death, you lose any materials that were in your inventory. You also lose all the experience points you had earned working and fighting. After you die in the game, you can choose to respawn. A standard respawn brings you back to life and sends you back to the same location where you started the game. If you want, you can also change your respawn point,

Don't worry if your character dies once in a while. You can always get back to where you were!

or change where you reappear, using a bed. You craft a bed from wood and sheep wool. Once you've slept in the bed, the bed's location becomes your new respawn point. Sleeping in a bed has another benefit, too: fast-forwarding the game through the night. Then the day comes much faster, and you can get right back to work!

When it was first released, *Minecraft* could only be played on a PC. However, Mojang later released Xbox and PlayStation versions of the game. They also created a mobile version called the Pocket Edition that works on tablets and smartphones. Each version of the game has some slight differences. The biggest change between them is the control scheme. Check your version's controls in the Options menu to familiarize yourself with the buttons and their actions. If you forget how to do something, you can always refer back to this menu by pausing the game.

Chapter 3

Getting Started

You've learned the basics, adventurer. Now it is time to enter the *Minecraft* world and put your creative skills and survival instincts to the test. Let's start a new game in Survival mode. Where did you spawn? Check your surroundings. You could be near an open field or a mountain. You may even spawn in the middle of a jungle! Each time you start a new game, the world will be different. That's part of the fun of *Minecraft*!

Thankfully, you are given a map to help you understand your surroundings. To look at the map, you first

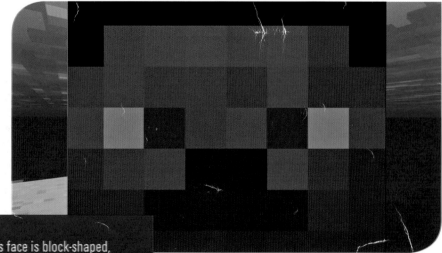

Your *Minecraft* character's face is block-shaped, just like everything else in the game!

need to Equip it, or move it from your backpack to your hands. Open your inventory window and select the map. Move it to the bottom row with nine slots. After you close your inventory, you can select the map to Equip it. Once you have Equipped the map, look down at your feet to read it. At the top of the map are **coordinates**. These measure your location in the world by X, Y, and Z. X shows how far west or east you are. Z shows how far north or south you are. Y shows how high up you are.

Let's make some tools. You won't survive long without these helpful items. First, you'll need

Check your map often to avoid getting lost.

Any kind of tree will do when you're looking for wood in the beginning of a new game.

some wood. Trees are usually close to any starting point, so try to find some. Hold the Mine button when you are near one. You will punch the tree trunk. As you punch it, you will see it start to break apart. It will eventually transform into a smaller, floating block that will fall to the ground. Simply move over the floating block of wood to collect it. Notice anything strange? The tree didn't fall over! Blocks in *Minecraft* are placed independently. This means you need to build on top of other blocks to make a tower, but

Punching trees will only get you so far before you need to think about getting better tools.

removing blocks from below will not cause the top to fall. Floating blocks! But be careful. A few types of blocks do fall down. These include sand and gravel.

Wooden tools are limited in use and don't last very long before breaking. But it's your first night in the *Minecraft* world, so we'll take what we can get. You can craft a few basic items by hand. However, a crafting table will enable you to craft much more. To make one, you'll need wood planks. Planks can be made from any type of wood—oak, birch, jungle wood, and others.

Open the Crafting menu. Placing wood blocks into one craft slot will allow you to make four plank blocks per wood block. Now we're getting somewhere! Place a wood plank in each of the four slots to craft a crafting table. Eureka! Place the table on the ground wherever you like. You can always move it later if you change your mind. Once the table is in place, press the Use button on it. This will open a new window. Here, your crafting area is bigger. This means you can craft bigger items.

Arrange two sticks and three wood planks in the shape of an ax in the crafting table screen. This will produce an ax. Try using your ax on another nearby tree trunk. You should notice that you are able to remove wood blocks quicker than by punching.

Crafting by Platform

Crafting can be slightly different depending on which version of the game you are playing. On the Xbox, PlayStation, and mobile versions, the Crafting menu is preloaded with the designs for crafting. You can pick the item you want to craft from a system of menus. In the PC version of the game, you will make the designs by hand in the Crafting menu. Throughout this book, you will find pictures showing how to craft different items in the PC version.

Just as in _Minecraft_, constructing houses and buildings requires careful planning and hard work from **engineers** and construction workers. The Empire State Building took 3,400 workers 410 days to build in 1931. Imagine what you could build in _Minecraft_ if you had 3,400 players helping you!

Keep an eye on the sun as you work. Once it begins to set, you should build a shelter. At sundown, harmful creatures come out. You need a place to hide from them for the night. Now that you have an ax to collect wood quickly and you know how to craft planks, building a wooden house shouldn't take long. You can build it anywhere you like. Since we're on a tight schedule, we'll keep the shelter very basic. Build the walls three or four blocks high. Your player is two blocks high, but a little extra room never hurts. Don't forget your crafting table. Keeping it in your house will make it easy to find.

What about an entrance? You can use the table to craft a door. Arrange planks in a shape that is two blocks wide and four blocks tall on the table. This creates a door measuring one block by two blocks. The door lets you get in and out of your house while keeping enemies out. A first shelter might look something like the picture below.

You can spend the night in your house or continue to explore during the night. It's up to you. Watch out, though! Because you don't have armor or weapons yet, the creatures of the night can be deadly.

Your first house might not be very fancy, but it will help you survive the night.

Chapter 4

What's Next?

id you make it through your first night in *Minecraft*? If so, congratulations! If not, don't feel bad. This was just your first try, and the first night is always the hardest. But you know how the game works, how to Equip and use tools, and how to build. It gets easier from here. Now, it's time to venture farther into the *Minecraft* world to discover its countless possibilities.

By this time, you are ready to start exploring. You have a couple of choices. If you are happy with your shelter's location, you can return there at night using the map. However, you can also collect the materials from your house and take them with you. Then you can rebuild it wherever you end up at sundown.

Your character may be getting hungry. This would be a good time to find some food. The most readily available foods are the animals around you. Cows, pigs, and chickens are easiest to find. A wooden sword will help you fight the animals. A sword can be made from two wooden planks and one stick. With the sword Equipped, you can obtain some meat for food.

Killing an animal will cause it to drop a few items. The items are a little different depending on the animal. For example, a chicken will drop a raw chicken, bones, and occasionally some feathers. The raw meat is food, and you can eat it by Equipping it and going through the Use action. You can eat the meat from these animals raw. However, raw pig meat has a risk of poisoning you temporarily. This slowly lowers your health until it wears off. Another option

Cows are an important source of meat in *Minecraft*.

Your heart meter will change color when your character is poisoned.

is to cook the meat using a furnace. You'll learn more about how to craft a furnace on pages 25 and 26.

Not every block is mined faster with an ax. Different tools are used for different materials. For tree trunks, use an ax. For dirt and gravel, use a shovel. Most block materials are hard rocks. They are best mined with the pickax. You can use the crafting table to make a wooden pickax from wooden planks and sticks.

Once you have a pickax, it is a good idea to **upgrade** your tools. The next best material for tools is cobblestone. Like wood, stone is a common resource. It can be found easily and mined in bulk. Stone blocks are gray. They can be found in caves or in areas such as mountains and cliffs. When broken with a pickax, they become cobblestone. Once you have some cobblestone, you can use it to make better tools. Stone tools will work even faster than wood ones. Better tools also let you mine a wider variety of materials.

Keeping a furnace and crafting table in your house makes it easier to produce the items you need.

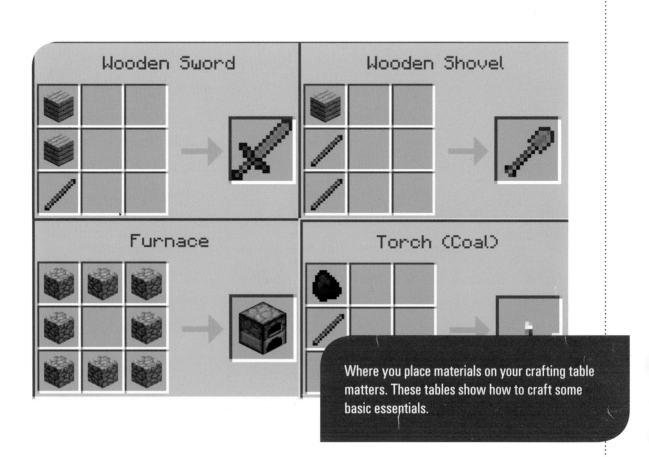

Where you place materials on your crafting table matters. These tables show how to craft some basic essentials.

As you mine stone, you may come across gray blocks with black spots. Those are coal blocks. When broken, they drop pieces of coal. Coal can be used to make torches and fuel furnaces. Later on, it can even power mine carts.

Along with upgrading tools, cobblestone can be used to make a furnace. A furnace is crafted from eight cobblestone blocks. It has many uses, such as creating ore or baking a cake. You can also use it to cook your raw meats. Cooked meat fills a larger portion of your food bar than raw meat does. Press the Use button on the furnace to open its cooking menu. Now you can choose food ingredients and fuel types. Furnaces need fuel to operate. Wood blocks and planks can be used here. Coal is a great fuel because it is common and lasts longer than wood. If you have not found coal yet, use wood planks as a fuel and wood blocks as an ingredient in your furnace. This will produce charcoal. Charcoal has the same uses as mined coal. Aside from powering a furnace, it can be used in dark caves to make torches. Torches can be crafted by hand from sticks and coal.

You may be running out of space in your inventory at this point. A good crafter uses chests to keep a clear inventory and stay organized. Chests can be crafted from eight wood planks. Placing a chest

Quick Tip: Mining Precaution

It is best not to dig straight down or straight up as you mine. Sand and gravel blocks fall when there is nothing to hold them up. If they fall on you, your character could get hurt or trapped. Also, you don't always know what lies beneath each block you mine. If you are above a cave, you could fall a great distance or even into lava when you break through the ceiling!

on the ground and using it will allow you to transfer items to it. In addition to organizing them, this also protects your items if your character dies. When you respawn, the chest and items will be right where you left them. A single chest has 27 item spaces, like your backpack. Two chests can be placed next to each other to make one large chest. These hold a combined total of 54 item spaces.

With torches, cooked food, and plenty of room in your inventory, you can more comfortably go into

You can place torches on walls to keep an entire area lit up.

caves in search of more **exotic** materials. Soon you will be finding iron and striking gold. An iron pickax can mine nearly any block in *Minecraft*. Caves are filled with many types of blocks to mine, and they are all usable in their own way. The hardest and most durable material is diamond. Diamonds are nearly as hard to find as they are to break. But with enough exploration, you can find the most precious gems deep under the surface.

What happens next is up to you! Maybe you've spotted a jungle you want to explore or a cave you want to venture into. The farther you go into the game, the more impressive the rewards become. But with the

Better armor and weapons will help you explore dangerous parts of the world.

Gold is a funny material in the game. It is rare, but tools made with gold are not very good. They are less powerful than stone tools, and they don't last long. The game was designed this way for a reason. In real life, pure gold is very soft compared to other metals. Gold jewelry or coins have other metals in them to make them hard. This means the gold in *Minecraft* is just like real gold. It might look nice, but it isn't very useful on its own.

rewards come more powerful enemies and more dangerous environments. There are places where only the bravest crafters go. There, they might fight flaming archers or swim in lava. Some crafters are even rumored to become dragon slayers! What do you want to do?

Glossary

coordinates (koh-OR-duh-nits) numbers used to show the position of a point on a line, graph, or map

engineers (en-juh-NEERZ) people who are specially trained to design and build machines or structures

exotic (ig-ZAH-tik) unusual and fascinating, or from a faraway place

inventory (IN-vuhn-tor-ee) a display of the items your character is carrying in *Minecraft*

ore (OR) rock or soil that contains metal or valuable minerals

precipitation (pri-sip-i-TAY-shun) the falling of water from the sky in the form of rain, sleet, hail, or snow

regenerate (rih-JEN-uh-rayt) to slowly recover on its own

upgrade (UP-grayd) to improve a piece of equipment or replace it with something better

Find Out More

BOOKS

Miller, Megan. *The Ultimate Unofficial Encyclopedia for Minecrafters: An A–Z of Tips and Tricks the Official Guides Don't Teach You*. New York, Skyhorse Publishing, Inc., 2015.

Milton, Stephanie, Paul Soares Jr., and Jordan Maron. *Minecraft: Essential Handbook*. New York: Scholastic, 2015.

O'Brien, Stephen. *The Ultimate Player's Guide to Minecraft*. Indianapolis, IN: Que Publishing, 2015.

WEB SITES

Minecraftopedia—How to Play Minecraft
www.minecraftopia.com/how_to_play_minecraft
This Web site offers tips and tricks on how to survive your first day (and night) in Minecraft.

Minecraft101—Getting Started with Minecraft
www.minecraft101.net/g/getting-started.html
If you need help with the bare bones of getting started, visit this site. It also has links to guides on other aspects of the game.

Index

About the Author

James Zeiger is a student at the Missouri University of Science and Technology. An avid gamer, his lifelong interest in engineering naturally led him to Minecraft.